# CENTRE OF THE EARTH

## RETOLD BY PAULINE FRANCIS

## EVANS BROTHERS LIMITED

Published by Evans Brothers Limited
2A Portman Mansions
Chiltern Street
London W1U 6NR

© Evans Brothers Limited 2003
First published 2003

Printed in Hong Kong

**British Library Cataloguing in Publication data**
Francis, Pauline
      Journey to the centre of the earth
      1. Adventure stories   2. Children's stories
      I. Title   II. Verne, Jules, 1828-1905
      823.9'14 [J]

ISBN 0237525348

VISIT OUR WEBSITE
Evans
www.evansbooks.co.uk

# JOURNEY TO THE CENTRE OF THE EARTH

# Introduction

Jules Verne was born in northern France in 1828. He went to study law in Paris, as his father had done. But as well as studying, he began to do what he really wanted – to write.

Jules Verne wrote several plays and some of them were performed on the Paris stage. In 1857, he married a widow with two young sons. He continued to work and write, because he had a family to support.

In 1862, Jules Verne wrote his first travel adventure, *Five Weeks in a Balloon*. It soon became very popular. From then on, Verne wrote for the same publisher, called Hetzel. In 1864, *Journey to the Centre of the Earth* was published. This book tells the story of Professor Lidenbrock and his nephew, Axel, who make a terrifying journey into an extinct volcano – right into the centre of the Earth. The book was made into a film in 1959.

Jules Verne wrote over sixty more novels before his death, in 1905. The best-known of these are *Twenty Thousand Leagues under the Sea* (1869) and *Around the World in Eighty Days* (1873).

# CHAPTER ONE
# *The strange parchment*

One Sunday morning at the end of May, my uncle, Professor Lidenbrock, came rushing back to his house half an hour earlier than usual. He flung down his hat and walking stick and went into his study.

"Axel!" he called. "Follow me."

I followed him, glancing around as I waited for him to speak. The study was like a museum, full of metals, minerals and rocks. My uncle was a Professor of Mineralogy at the nearby university.

"I found this in a bookshop this morning!" he said at last, holding up a huge old book. "Isn't it beautiful?"

"Splendid!" I replied, trying to sound enthusiastic. "What is this wonderful book about?"

"This book," my uncle replied excitedly, "is by a famous Icelandic writer from the twelfth century."

"Is it a translation?" I asked.

"What?" he roared. "What would I be doing with a translation? It is in Icelandic, written in the alphabet once used in that country. Come and look!"

I was just leaning over the book to see these strange letters when a dirty piece of parchment slipped from its pages on to the floor. My uncle picked it up and unfolded it carefully. It was covered with columns of letters I did not recognise. He took out his magnifying glass and started to examine them.

"Sit down, Axel," he said. "I am going to call out the letters as they would be in our alphabet. Write them down carefully." This is what I wrote:

| mm.rnlls | esreuel | seecJde |
| sgtssmf | unteief | niedrke |
| kt,samn | atrateS | Saodrrn |
| emtnaeI | nuaect | rrilSa |
| Atvaar | .nscrc | ieaabs |
| ccdrmi | eeutul | frantu |
| dt,iac | oseibo | KediiY |

"The first letter is a double m," my uncle said, "and that wasn't added to the Icelandic language until two

hundred years after this book was written. One of the book's owners must have left it here. But who?"

My uncle examined the book carefully once more. On the back of the second page was a stain like an inkblot. He studied it closely. "Arne Saknussemm!" he cried in triumph. "A famous Icelandic scientist from the sixteenth century!"

He looked at the words I had written for him. "They would make sense if I knew how to rearrange them," he muttered. "I shall not eat or sleep until I discover what they mean. Nor will you, Axel!"

As I stood there, I glanced at the portrait of Gräuben on the wall. Gräuben was a charming girl with blue eyes and blonde hair, and I loved her dearly. My uncle was her guardian, but he did not know that we were secretly engaged. Suddenly, my uncle thumped the table with his fist and brought me back down to earth.

"What if the letters were written down the page instead of across it!" he cried. "Write a sentence, Axel, down the page, in five or six columns." I wrote:

| I | o | m | y | i | r |
|---|---|---|---|---|---|
| l | u | u | d | t | ä |
| o | v | c | e | t | u |
| v | e | h | a | l | b |
| e | r | , | r | e | e |
| y | y | m | l | G | n |

7

"Now write it out, reading each line across," my uncle said. I obeyed, with the following result:

*Iomyir luudtä ovcetu vehalb er,ree yymlGn*

"Splendid!" my uncle cried, snatching the paper out of my hand. "Now all I have to do is to read the first letter of each word, then the second letter of each word, and so on." And to his great surprise – and mine – he read out: "I love you very much, my dear little Gräuben."

"Is this true, Axel?"

"Yes, er, no!" I replied, confused.

Luckily, my uncle was more interested in the mysterious code. "Well," he said, "let's apply my method to the parchment."

My uncle gave a loud cough and started to read the letters as he had done mine:

*mmessunkaSenrA.icefdoK.segnittamurtn*
*ecertserrette,rotaivsadua,ednecsedsadne*
*lacartniiiluJsiratracSarbmutabiledmek*
*meretarcsilucoYsleffenSnI*

"It still doesn't make sense!" he shouted angrily.

He ran from his study and disappeared through the front door as fast as his legs would carry him. After he had gone, I began to think about the words I had written down from the parchment. I picked them up and studied them for a long time. I fanned myself with the piece of paper, gazing at the strange words as they floated for a moment before my eyes. That moment told me the secret! I read out the whole sentence aloud – backwards!

"Oh no!" I cried, trembling with terror. "If I tell my uncle what the parchment says, he will want to go straight away. Nothing will stop him. He will take me and we will never come back! I shall not tell him what I have found out."

When my uncle came back, he worked on the code through the night and most of the next day. By two o'clock in the afternoon, I gave in. Hunger had beaten me. "Uncle," I began, "yesterday, by chance…"

I handed him the sheet of paper on which I had copied the rearranged words, first in Latin, then in German. My uncle read it quickly. When he had finished, he jumped into the air as if he had received an electric shock. Then he sank into his armchair. "Let's have something to eat," he said, "then you can pack my bags." He paused for a minute. "And your own!"

At his words, a shudder went through my body. I picked up the piece of paper and read it again:

*Descend into the volcanic crater of Sneffells Yokul, brave traveller, over which the shadow of Scartaris falls at the end of June, and you will reach the centre of the earth. I have done this.*

*Arne Saknussemm*

## CHAPTER TWO
# *We reach Iceland*

I decided to try to stop my uncle. "There is nothing to prove that the parchment is genuine," I said. "Perhaps Arne Saknussemm is playing a joke."

"A joke!" my uncle cried. "He was a famous man in the sixteenth century. He travelled all over the world."

"I have never heard of the names, Yokul and Sneffells," I went on.

"Take down the third atlas on the fourth shelf," he replied. "It has the best map of Iceland."

I did as he asked and found the map.

"You can see that there are volcanoes all over Iceland," he said. "Yokul means glacier in Icelandic. Most volcanic eruptions in Iceland must push through the layers of ice in the glaciers. So the word is also used to describe the volcanoes in that country."

He traced his finger north along the west coast of Iceland. "That is Sneffells," he announced, "and this is Scartaris, one of its peaks. It will become the most famous volcano in the world if its crater leads to the centre of the Earth."

"But that's impossible!" I cried, "the crater must be full of lava and burning rocks and…"

"Sneffells is an extinct volcano. It has not erupted since 1229," my uncle told me calmly.

"All right," I said, "this man, Saknussemm, he may have gone into the crater, he may have seen the shadow of Scartaris touch it, but he could not have reached the centre of the Earth and come back alive!"

"And why not?" asked my uncle, crossly.

"Scientists know that for every seventy feet below the Earth's surface, the temperature rises about one degree," I said. "So we know that the temperature at the centre of the Earth must be over two million degrees."

"And so you are afraid of melting away?" my uncle laughed. "Nobody really knows what is going on inside the Earth. We might discover that the scientists were wrong. In any case," he said, "we shall see for ourselves."

I came out of my uncle's study in a daze. Was my uncle a madman or a genius? I decided to go for a walk, and as I walked, I caught sight of Gräuben.

"What's the matter, Axel?" she asked, noticing the worried expression on my face.

I told her. For a few moments, she remained silent. "Axel," she said at last. "It will be a wonderful journey, a journey worthy of a scientist's nephew."

"You mean, you want me to go?" I cried.

Gräuben nodded and I, tired out by the day's emotions, said no more about it.

"It's only May," I told myself. "The end of June is a long way off. Many things could change my uncle's mind by then." But when I reached home, he was packing.

"Are we going, then?" I murmured.

"Yes, you idiot!" he cried. "The day after tomorrow. It is not easy to get to Iceland from Germany!"

Our journey was long and slow. As soon as we had reached Denmark, my uncle searched the harbour in Copenhagen for a ship that would take us to Iceland. To my great disappointment, there was one leaving almost immediately. We left port on 2 June and arrived in Iceland ten days later. Before we left the ship, my uncle dragged me on to the deck and pointed to a high mountain with a double snow-covered peak. "That is Sneffells!" he cried. "Things are going well."

On 16 June, at five o'clock in the morning, the neighing of four horses under my window woke me up. I dressed quickly and went down into the street. Our Icelandic guide, Hans, was loading the last of our luggage. An hour later, everything was ready. We climbed on to our horses and set off under a cloudy sky. At first, the pleasure of riding put me in a good mood. "Where's the risk in visiting an extinct volcano?" I asked myself.

Days later, we reached the foot of Sneffells.

"When we get to the top, I shall explore the crater as far down as I can go," my uncle explained to Hans.

As I heard him say this, I was filled with fear again. "If that madman Saknussemm was speaking the truth," I whispered to myself, "then we are going to get lost inside the Earth. There is no proof that Sneffells is extinct. Just because it has been asleep for more than five hundred years doesn't mean it will never wake up again!"

## CHAPTER THREE
# *Inside the crater*

Sneffells is five thousand feet high. We walked in single file, led by Hans. In spite of my terror, I was fascinated by the volcanic rocks I could see all around me.

The ground began to rise sharply. Hans walked as calmly as if he were still on level ground. The small stones kept rolling down the mountainside, but the larger ones made a sort of staircase which helped us to climb. By seven o'clock in the evening, we had climbed three thousand feet. It was bitterly cold and the wind was blowing hard. I was exhausted. In spite of his impatience, my uncle decided to stop. But Hans shook his head.

"Mistour!" he shouted.

"What does he mean?" I asked anxiously.

My uncle pointed. In the distance, I saw a column of powdered dust and stone, twisting and turning like a waterspout and coming towards us. Hans quickly led us to safety on the other side of the mountain. We decided to carry on after that. Five hours later, in complete darkness, we reached the top of Sneffells.

That night, I slept better than I had done for a long time, in spite of the hard rock beneath me. The next morning, we awoke half frozen by the cold air, although

the sun shone brightly. I stood up and looked around me. It was so beautiful! I could see deep valleys criss-crossing the land far below, glaciers and other peaks, and the endless sea. Then I forced myself to look down. The opening in the crater of Sneffells was about one mile wide and about two thousand feet deep. "The bottom will be filled with thunder and flames!" I whispered to myself, "only a madman would go down there."

But there was no going back. Hans set off and I followed him without a word. By noon, we had arrived at the bottom of the slope leading to the crater. There were three holes in the crater, each about a hundred feet wide. They yawned open at our feet and I did not have the courage to look into them. But my uncle ran from one to the other, waving and muttering. Then he stopped to stare at a large rock in the middle of the crater. Suddenly, he gave a shout.

"Axel! Axel! Come here!" he cried. I ran over to him.

"Look!" my uncle said.

I recognised the letters from the old book. It was Arne Saknussemm's name.

"Do you believe me now?" my uncle cried. "All we have to do is wait for the shadow of Scartaris to touch the edge of one of the holes, and we shall know where to go. Now we must sleep and wait for the sun to rise."

The next few days were cloudy and I felt hopeful.

"If the sun does not appear soon, we shall have to wait another year!" my uncle shouted angrily.

But to my disappointment, the sun came out the next day, pouring its rays into the crater. The peak of Scartaris stood out sharply above our heads. At midday, its shadow touched the edge of the middle hole.

"That's the one!" my uncle cried. "Now for the centre of the Earth!"

The time had come for me to look into that bottomless pit. I did not want to seem cowardly in front of the others. I walked forward and peered down. "Even if we get down using our ropes, how will we unfasten them when we arrive at the other end?" I asked myself.

My uncle had already thought about this problem. He took out a piece of rope four hundred feet long. "I shall let down half of this," he explained, "and loop it over a piece of lava here at the top. Then I shall throw the other half down. We shall each descend by holding both halves of the rope. When we are two hundred feet down, we shall be able to take down all the rope by letting go of one end and pulling the other! Then we shall do the same all over again... until..." He looked at me. "...until we reach the centre of the Earth."

We began to descend into the hole. Hans first, then my uncle – and then me! After half an hour, we reached a large rock protruding from the side of the shaft. Hans pulled down the rope and we set off again. All the way down, my uncle looked at the rocks closely.

"I am sure that the English scientist was right," he said. "There is no heat inside the Earth."

"We have been going down for nearly eleven hours," I gasped. "I calculate that we have dropped nearly three thousand feet."

As I spoke, Hans stopped. "Halt!" he cried.

"We have arrived at the bottom!" my uncle called up.

"Is there a way out?" I shouted back.

"Yes," he answered. "There's a sort of tunnel slanting away to the right."

We spent the night there. Lying on my back, I saw a bright star at the end of the shaft. Then I fell into a deep sleep. At eight o'clock the next morning, a ray of daylight woke me, and I got up.

"Now, Axel," my uncle said. "We really are going to plunge under the Earth."

He pulled me after him, excitedly.

"This then is the precise moment at which our journey begins."

## CHAPTER FOUR
# *A dead end*

My uncle fixed up a lamp around his neck.

"Forward!" he cried.

As I plunged into the gloomy passage behind him, I glanced up and caught a last glimpse of the Icelandic sky.

"I shall never see it again," I whispered to myself.

The tunnel sloped down sharply and we let the baggage slide in front of us at the end of a long rope. I kept looking at the thermometer as we went down.

"Only four degrees warmer," I said in surprise. "Perhaps we are going across rather than down!"

We walked for more than seven hours. At last, we sat down to eat. "Uncle Lidenbrock, there is only enough water left for a few days," I told him.

"Don't worry, Axel," he smiled, "we shall find more when we have gone through this bed of lava."

"But we cannot have gone down more than a thousand feet," I said. "The temperature has risen by only a few degrees."

"According to my calculations," my uncle said, "we are now ten thousand feet below sea-level."

"So the temperature should be eighty-one degrees!" I cried. "It is only fifteen! How do you explain that?"

He did not answer.

The next day, at six o'clock in the morning, we set off again. Six hours later, we came to a place where two paths crossed. They were both dark and narrow.

"Which one shall we take?" I asked.

My uncle pointed to the east path. I do not know why. Perhaps he did not want to hesitate in front of us. The slope of this new path was very slight. Along the way were arches of lava, some very high and others very low. Sometimes we had to crawl. Then, suddenly, the ground seemed to rise in front of us.

"If we keep on like this," I told my uncle, "we shall arrive back at the surface."

He shrugged his shoulders and did not speak as he carried on. I followed, afraid of being left behind. The lava gave way to rocks such as slate and limestone.

"Look, uncle!" I cried, "we have come to the rocks that were formed when the first plants and animals appeared on Earth."

I expected him to look surprised. But he walked on without saying a word.

"Perhaps he knows he has made a mistake by choosing this tunnel," I thought. "Or have I made a mistake about the rocks?" I walked on. "If I am right," I muttered, "then I should find the remains of some animals or plants."

I had not gone more than a hundred yards when I felt that I was walking on some kind of dust. "This is from plants or animals!" I said, overjoyed. I could not stand my uncle's silence any longer. I picked up a perfectly preserved shell, which had belonged to a tiny animal, and ran after him.

"Look at this!" I cried.

"Yes, we have left the lava behind," he said. "I may have made a mistake, but I cannot be sure until we reach the end of the tunnel."

"But we are in danger!" I said.

"What of, Axel?" he asked.

"Dying of thirst!" I told him. "There is only enough water left for three days."

We walked the whole of the next day. The rocks sparkled in the light of the lamp and I saw in them the remains of reptiles, from a later age than the ones we had seen the day before. By the end of the next day, the glossy rocks had given way to a dark, dull rock. As the tunnel narrowed, I looked at it closely. It was coal.

Soon, we came to an enormous cavern, a hundred feet wide and one hundred and fifty feet high. We trudged through it all day.

"It is never coming to an end," I gasped, thirsty and exhausted. I spoke too soon. Suddenly, right in front of us, loomed a wall. We had come to a dead end.

"Now at least we know," my uncle said. "This is not the path that Saknussemm took. There's nothing we can do but turn back. In less than three days, we can be back at the other path."

"But we have no water left!" I cried.

# CHAPTER FIVE
# *Water everywhere!*

It was a hard journey back. My uncle did not complain because he was angry with himself. Hans was as calm as ever. I grumbled loudly. We had nothing to drink by the end of the first day, except for some gin. More than once, I nearly fainted from heat and tiredness.

At last, on Tuesday 7 July, we arrived once again at the junction with the other path. We were on our hands and knees, half-dead. I lay down on the lava floor, groaning.

"Poor child!" my uncle said gently.

I took his trembling hands in mine. He let me hold them and looked at me with tears in his eyes. Then I saw him take a flask from his belt and hold it to my lips.

"Drink this water," he said. "It's the last, the very last. I kept it for you, Axel."

"Thank you!" I cried. Some of my strength came back to me. "We must go back up," I whispered, "or we shall all die."

My uncle did not look at me. A long silence followed. "Go back?" he said, at last. "No, Hans will take you back. I shall go on alone."

I wished then that Hans and I could speak the same language. Then together we could have made my uncle see sense. I went over to him and pointed to the path leading back to the shaft. But he gently shook his head and pointed to my uncle.

"My master," he said, in his language.

"No, you fool!" I cried. "We must take him back with us! Don't you understand?"

I tried to force Hans to get up. While I was struggling with him, my uncle came over to us.

"Calm down, Axel," he said. "I have another idea. There must be water in the other tunnel. While you were resting just now, I went to look. That tunnel plunges straight down towards the centre of the Earth. There will be springs of water there. I am asking you for one day, that is all. If we do not find the water we need, I swear to you that we will return to the surface."

I was touched by his promise. "I shall do as you wish," I told him. "Let us be on our way."

We went into the new tunnel. My uncle held his lamp up to the walls. "When the Earth began to cool down," he said, "the cooling produced cracks in the rocks. We are walking along one of these. You can see layers of minerals – copper, manganese, platinum, and even some gold. As we go down, we shall see mica, then granite."

He was right. Further down, the flakes of white mica dazzled our eyes. Then, suddenly, the rocks darkened and we were surrounded by gloomy granite. It was now eight o'clock in the evening and there was no sign of water. My legs began to tremble. I gave a cry and fell.

"Help!" I cried. "I am dying!"

My uncle turned back. He looked down at me with his arms folded. "It is all over," he muttered angrily.

The last thing I saw before I closed my eyes was his angry face. When I opened them again, I saw Hans and my uncle sleeping on the ground.

"We are all going to die," I whispered. "It is four miles to the surface. We are too weak to go back now."

A few hours went by. As I lay there half-asleep, I heard a noise. I thought I could see Hans in the distance, holding up a lamp.

"Hans has left us!" I tried to shout to my uncle, but my mouth was so dry that the words did not come out.

I lay there for another hour, feeling that I would go mad. But then I heard Hans coming back. He woke up my uncle. "Vatten," he said.

"Water! Water!" I cried, clapping my hands.

We got ready quickly and made our way down a steep slope. Through the granite walls, I could hear a sort of dull rumbling, like distant thunder.

"There is an underground river flowing around us," my uncle said excitedly.

But as we went on further, the sound grew fainter. We turned back to the place where the water had sounded so clearly. I sat next to the wall. I could hear water rushing past on the other side. Hans took hold of his pickaxe and attacked the rock. Soon, a small opening appeared in the granite. Hans worked for more than an hour, cutting further and further into the rock. Suddenly a jet of water shot from the hole on to the opposite wall. Hans cried out with pain as the water hit him. I put out my hand and cried out, too.

"It is boiling hot!" I shouted.

"It will cool down," my uncle replied calmly.

The tunnel filled with steam as the water ran away into the tunnel. We took our first mouthful of water. We did not care where it had come from, or even whether it was safe to drink.

"We must fill the water-bottles and flasks," I said.

"And since the water is running downwards, it will guide us as well as refresh us," my uncle replied.

We followed the stream for days. I hardly thought any longer about the sun, stars and the moon, or trees, houses and towns. My uncle took hourly readings from his instruments. I was amazed when I read his calculations.

"If you are correct, uncle," I said, "then we are two hundred and thirteen miles east of our starting point and forty-eight miles under the Atlantic Ocean. The temperature ought to be one thousand five hundred degrees and the granite ought to be melting!"

"As you can see for yourself, it isn't," he laughed. "But you are right about the ocean above us."

I shuddered. At this moment, above our heads, ships were being tossed about by the waves and whales were knocking their tails on the roof of our prison!

## CHAPTER SIX
# *Lost in the dark*

By 7 August, we were about seventy-five miles below the Earth's surface. I was walking in front of the others, holding one of the lamps, when I turned round and saw that I was alone.

"I must go back and join the others," I told myself.

I walked the way I had come for a quarter of an hour. I called out, but my voice just echoed around the walls of the tunnel. A shiver ran down my spine.

"Keep calm, Axel," I said over and over again. "There is only one path so I shall find them again."

I walked on in a terrible silence. At last, I stopped.

"How can I still be alone?" I thought. "I cannot be lost because I am following the stream."

I bent down to plunge my hands and face into the river. To my astonishment, I was standing on rough, dry granite. The stream had disappeared. There are no words to describe how I felt at that moment.

"I am buried alive!" I wept, "and I shall die from hunger and thirst."

I touched the dry rock once again. Why had I not noticed that the ground was dry when I turned back? There must have been a fork in the tunnel at that point!

How could I get back there now? There were no footprints on the hard ground.

I was lost.

I started to think about Gräuben, then about my mother who had died when I was very young. I knelt down to pray for a while. At last, I got up.

"I must look for the stream again," I told myself. "Even if I cannot find Hans and my uncle, I might be able to get back to the surface again. I have enough water in my flask for three days."

I started to walk back along the steep tunnel. I did not recognise anything along the way. Suddenly, it came to a dead end. I fell on to the floor, crying in despair. My

lamp, damaged in the fall, began to dim. Moving shadows flickered across the walls. I stared at the lamp until it went out and I was plunged into total darkness. A terrible cry burst from my lips.

At this point, I went mad. I stood up with my arms stretched out in front of me, trying to feel my way. I ran downwards through the Earth's crust, crying and shouting. I bruised myself on the jagged rocks. I kept falling and getting up again. After several hours, I fell exhausted on to the floor and lost consciousness. When I came round again, my face was wet with tears and I was covered in blood. I rolled myself across the floor and curled up against the opposite wall. Just as I was hoping to die there quickly, a loud noise struck my ears. It was like a roll of thunder.

After a long silence, I could hear voices on the other side of the wall. It was Hans or my uncle. And if I could hear them, they could hear me.

"Help!" I cried with all my strength. "Help!"

I listened for a reply. There was nothing to be heard. I listened again. I moved my ear along the wall and the sound seemed clearer.

"That wall is solid granite," I said to myself, "no sound could come through it. This noise is coming along the tunnel itself."

I listened again. This time I heard my name.

"I must speak along the wall if I want them to hear me," I thought. I went closer to the wall.

"Uncle Lidenbrock!" I said as clearly as possible.

"Axel! Axel! Is that you?" my uncle shouted back.

"Yes!" I said. "Lost in the dark. The lamp is broken and the stream has disappeared."

"Oh, I have wept for you, my poor boy," he said. "Now I am going to measure the time between your call and my reply so that we know how far apart we are."

As soon as his voice reached me, I spoke back.

"Forty seconds," he called. "So the sound took twenty seconds to cover the distance between us. Sound travels at just over a thousand feet a second. We're nearly four miles apart."

"Should I go up or down?" I asked.

"Down," he told me. "We are in a huge cave with many tunnels leading into it. Now get up and start walking, my boy."

"Goodbye, uncle!" I called. "I'm leaving now."

The slope was steep and I let myself slide most of the way. But the steepness was so alarming that I was almost falling. I no longer had the strength to stop myself. Suddenly, the ground disappeared from under my feet. As I fell, I bounced off the rocky walls of the tunnel. Then my head hit a sharp rock.

I lost consciousness.

## CHAPTER SEVEN

# *An underground sea*

When I came round again, I lay on a thick rug in the half-darkness. As I opened my eyes, I saw my uncle leaning over me. He took my hand and gave a cry of joy. "He's alive!" he cried. "My dear boy, you are safe!"

I was deeply touched by the affection in his voice, and the joy also in Hans's voice as he greeted me.

"And now, uncle," I said, "tell me where we are."

"Tomorrow, Axel," he said, "you must sleep now."

"At least tell me what time and day it is," I begged.

"It is eleven o'clock at night and today is Sunday, 9 August," he told me.

I closed my eyes and let myself drop off to sleep. In the morning, when I woke up, I stared around me in amazement. I was in a large cave decorated by stalagmites and carpeted with fine sand. It was half-light.

"There is no lamp burning," I thought, "but there seems to be light coming from somewhere. And I'm sure I can hear the wind blowing, and the sound of water."

My uncle came over to me. "Good morning, Axel," he said brightly, "I can see that you are feeling better."

"Yes, I am," I replied, sitting up. "Now tell me what has happened."

"It is a miracle that you were not killed," my uncle said. "You fell to the bottom of a shaft along with many large pieces of rock. Any one of them could have crushed you."

"Has my brain been affected?" I asked. "I can hear the wind and the sea."

"I shall show you," he said, "but I want you to feel better first. Our voyage will be a long one, I think."

"Our voyage?" I asked.

"Yes," he replied. "Rest today and we will set sail tomorrow."

"Set sail?" I cried. "But that means there is a river or a lake or a sea outside! I must see it straight away!"

My uncle gave in and took me outside the cave. At first I saw nothing. My eyes were not used to the light. A few minutes later, I could see more clearly. An enormous sheet of water stretched as far as I could see. At its edge was a beach of fine golden sand. From this gently sloping beach rose high cliffs.

"The sea!" I cried happily.

"I have named it the Lidenbrock, after myself," my uncle smiled.

"The light is different," I said. "This is not the light of the sun or the moon. It has no warmth."

My uncle nodded. "Yes, Axel," he said. "We are inside a cave big enough to contain a sea. It must be several miles high. Its ceiling must be resting on those granite cliffs we can see over there."

I gazed at this wonder in silence, unable to find the words to express my feelings.

"I feel as if I am on another planet," I thought.

My uncle took my arm and we walked along the beach. To our left, waterfalls cascaded down the cliffs. A few clouds of light steam passing from one rock to the other told us there were hot springs. Ahead of us stood thousands of trees, thirty or forty feet high, which did not move at all in the wind.

"It's a forest of giant mushrooms!" my uncle laughed as we came nearer.

We walked through this damp, fleshy forest. We were pleased to reach the other side. There we came across huge ferns and cacti.

"Astonishing!" my uncle cried. "These are our humble garden plants but at an earlier stage, when they used to be trees! What a feast for the eyes!"

"There could be animals, too," he said, looking down. "There are bones scattered everywhere."

I examined some of the skeletons. "I do not understand," I told my uncle. "Animal life only existed on Earth when there was soil on the Earth's surface."

"Well, Axel," my uncle said. "There is a very simple answer. This is that soil."

"What!" I cried, "eighty-eight miles below the ground?"

"Yes," he said. "A long time ago, the Earth's crust was very elastic and it moved up and down. Some of the soil on the surface was carried to the bottom of the cracks that suddenly opened up."

"What is above us, uncle?" I asked.

He consulted his notebooks. "We are eight hundred and seventy-five miles from Iceland," he said. "The mountains of Scotland are above our head right now."

"What if…?" I began.

"The ceiling is strong enough to hold them," he laughed.

"Are you thinking of returning to the Earth's surface soon?" I asked.

"Returning!" my uncle cried. "Certainly not! As everything is going so well, we shall go on. All oceans on the surface are really lakes since they are surrounded by land. There is no reason why it is not the same down here. I am sure we shall find new tunnels on the opposite shore. Now we must set sail. Hans is already hard at work building a raft."

"How wide is the sea, do you think?" I whispered.

"About eighty or a hundred miles across," he replied.

My heart sank. My uncle had been wrong before. What if he was wrong again?

## CHAPTER EIGHT
# *A battle of monsters*

We set sail the next morning. Just as we were leaving the little harbour, my uncle caught my arm.

"We shall call it Port Axel," he said.

"I have a better name for it," I said. "Port Gräuben."

A vast sea stretched before my eyes. As the shore disappeared from our sight, I began to keep a diary of our journey.

**Friday, 14 August**

Weather fine and warm. Hans catches a fish, a fish that is now found only in fossils on the Earth's surface.

**Saturday, 15 August**

Uncle Lidenbrock is anxious. The sea is wider than he first thought. Have we come the wrong way again?

**Sunday, 16 August**

Hans ties one of the heaviest pickaxes to a rope and lets it into the water to see how deep it is. It is difficult to pull it back up. I see that there are strange marks on the metal – like teeth marks! Are they the teeth of some prehistoric monster?

## Monday, 17 August

Today I try to remember the monsters that roamed the Earth in the Jurassic Age, before mammals. No human eye has ever seen them alive, but I have seen their skeletons in a museum. One was thirty feet long!

I gaze in terror at the sea. I check that the guns are in good condition. The surface of the water has been moving. Danger is near.

## Tuesday, 18 August

I fall asleep when Hans is on watch. Two hours later, a violent shock awakes me. The raft has been lifted out of the water and flung into the air. As we come back down, we can see huge dark shapes in the distance, blowing out water high into the air. We are horrified by this herd of enormous sea monsters. The smallest of them could break the raft with one snap of its jaws.

Hans wants to turn and sail away from them. But in the opposite direction we see other monsters. We are in the middle.

As the monsters come closer, they move the raft at greater speed in narrowing circles. We are speechless with fright. I pick up my rifle and get ready to shoot, but Hans shakes his head. The monsters pass within a hundred yards of the raft and hurl themselves on one another so angrily that they do not see us.

The battle begins. My uncle picks up his telescope and looks closely. "There are only two monsters!" he cries. "The first has the snout of a porpoise, the head of a lizard and a crocodile's teeth. It is an ichthyosaurus!"

"And the other?" I ask.

"A serpent with a turtle's shell – the plesiosaurus."

These two animals attack each other with terrible anger. As they fight, they make waves as high as mountains. Suddenly, they disappear under the water. We wait. Then the head of the plesiosaurus shoots out of the water. Its bleeding neck twists and writhes, lashing the waves like a gigantic whip. Soon, its long body stretches out upon the calm water. We cannot see the ichthyosaurus. Will it come back for us?

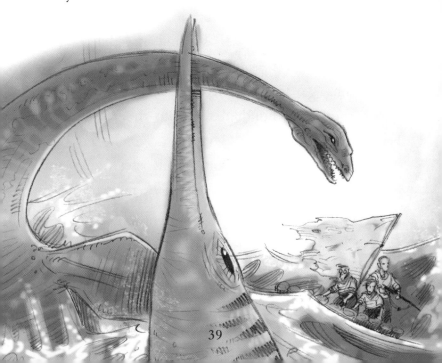

## CHAPTER NINE
# *The storm*

**Wednesday, 19 August**

A strong wind helps us to get away quickly from yesterday's battle scene.

**Thursday, 20 August**

Today there is a new danger. We can hear a loud roar in the distance and I am afraid that it may be a great waterfall. But such a lot of water would produce a strong current and the sea is completely calm. I throw an empty bottle into the sea but it lies still...

At four o'clock in the afternoon, Hans points to the south. A huge jet of water is rising into the air. What monster could make such a thing? By eight o'clock in the evening, we are only five miles away from the water which spurts five hundred feet into the air. Suddenly, Hans laughs and shouts, "Geyser!"

The geyser is truly magnificent. It rises from a small island and sparkles like a rainbow as the ray of electricity mingles with the water.

**Friday, 21 August**

Dark clouds surround us. The atmosphere is so full of

electricity that my hair is standing on end. For a moment, the wind stops completely. Then, suddenly, it blows with the strength of a hurricane and I can hardly write this down. The raft is rising into the air, its sail billowing out like a bubble about to burst…

The rain is falling like a waterfall in front of us. The sea becomes rough as brilliant flashes of lightning mingle with the rolls of thunder. Hailstones strike us. The bright light dazzles me and the noise of the thunder deafens me. I cling to the mast, which bends like a reed before the violence of the storm.

## Sunday, 23 August
Where are we? Last night was terrible and the storm has not yet gone. It is so noisy that we cannot speak. Zigzags of lightning hurl downwards, then shoot up to the granite ceiling. It is getting hotter.

## Monday, 24 August
Will this never end? We are utterly worn out, but Hans is as calm as ever. The raft is still heading southeast and we have travelled more than five hundred miles from the geyser.

At midday, the storm grows worse and we have to tie everything to the raft, including ourselves. Suddenly a ball of fire comes towards us. The sail and the mast vanish together, rising into the air like a prehistoric bird.

We are paralysed with fear. The fireball, half white and half blue, moves slowly over the raft. I sit, pale and trembling, under its hot glare. I try to move, but I cannot. A smell of gas fills the air so that we can hardly breathe. Suddenly there is a blaze of light as the ball bursts. Then everything goes dark.

## Tuesday, 25 August

I have just opened my eyes again. The storm is still raging. I can hear a new noise! I think it is the sound of the sea breaking on rocks! But...

My diary ended there.

When the raft hit the rocks, I remember being flung into the sea. I would have been torn to pieces if Hans had not carried me to the beach. I found myself lying there next to my uncle. We all fell into a painful sleep.

The next day, the weather was wonderful. My uncle was in good spirits. "We've arrived, my boy!" he smiled.

"At the end of our journey?" I asked hopefully.

"No," he replied, "at the end of the sea. Now we can plunge down into the Earth again."

"Uncle, what about our return journey?" I whispered.

"Simple!" he declared. "Once we have reached the centre of the Earth, we shall find a new way to the surface. If not, we shall go back the way we came."

Hans had spread out all our belongings on the sand.

"We have enough biscuits, salt meat, gin and dried fish for four months," I said.

"Four months!" my uncle cried. "We have time to get there and back! And I shall give a dinner for all my colleagues in Germany with what is left."

## CHAPTER TEN
# *Through the volcano*

"We leave in the morning!" announced my uncle, "and meanwhile, we shall explore this part of the coast while Hans is repairing the raft."

We walked together along the shores of the Lidenbrock Sea. Suddenly, after about a mile, we came to a plain covered with enormous mounds of bones. It looked like a huge cemetery. It was an amazing collection of every prehistoric animal and human being known to man. Suddenly, I stopped.

"There are animals moving about," I whispered.

"They're mastodons!" my uncle replied, his face amazed. "They were very similar to mammoths, but they had different teeth. We must get closer."

I shook my head. "It is not safe for humans," I said.

"You are wrong, Axel," he said. "I can see a man leaning against one of the trees."

I looked to where he was pointing. This man was over twelve feet tall. His head, which was as big as a buffalo's, was half-hidden under his tangled hair. He was holding a huge branch as he watched over his animals.

"Come on!" I cried to my uncle, "run!"

For the first time in his life, he obeyed me. We left the

forest, overcome by amazement at what we had seen. Was that creature really a man or simply an animal that looked like a human being? We did not know.

As we went on, I saw something shining in the sand. I ran to pick it up.

"A dagger!" I cried, holding it up for my uncle to see.

My uncle looked at it. "Axel," he said, excitedly, "this dagger is the sort that people used to carry in the sixteenth century. And from the marks on the blade it has been used to carve into rock. Let us look around."

We searched the foot of the cliffs, reaching a place where the beach narrowed. Between two rocks we caught sight of the entrance to a dark tunnel. There, on a slab of granite were two letters: A.S.

"Arne Saknussemm!" my uncle cried.

I stood still with surprise. There was no doubt now. The man who left that strange parchment really existed and he really had made this journey. I forgot all the dangers we had faced. "Forward!" I cried excitedly, rushing into the tunnel.

"Let us fetch Hans and the raft first," my uncle laughed.

It was six o'clock in the evening by the time we all stood inside the tunnel. But we soon found our way blocked by an enormous rock, which must have rolled down long after Saknussemm's visit.

"We cannot go back now!" I cried. "I shall blow up the rock."

We made a hole in the rock and I filled it with gunpowder before going to sleep. Even now, I cannot think of the next day, 27 August, without my heart beating with fear. That morning, I lit the trail of powder leading inside the tunnel. Then I ran back to my uncle and Hans who were waiting on the raft.

As the rock exploded inside the tunnel, I saw an enormous hole open in front of us. I felt the raft move, and heard a roar of water as we were carried on a huge wave into the chasm. We rushed down in complete darkness at first. Then Hans managed to light a candle. We could see that we were in a wide shaft.

"Saknussemm must have climbed down here," my uncle said.

We clung to the raft's mast. Most of our food and ropes had been swept away. Suddenly, the candle flickered and went out. Like a child, I closed my eyes to keep out the danger and the darkness. Much, much later, silence took the place of the roaring.

"We are going up now!" my uncle shouted. "The lamp! Light the lamp!" In the dim light, we could see that we were in a narrow shaft, about twenty feet across.

"The water has reached the bottom of the abyss," my uncle explained. "Now it is rising and taking us with it."

"Where to?" I asked. But he did not know.

We were rising fast and it was getting hotter. "The water beneath us is boiling!" I cried. In the distance, I could hear loud noises and rumblings, like rolls of thunder. "Uncle!" I shouted. "We are all going to die!"

"Axel," he replied. "We are in the crater of a volcano. It is the best thing that can happen to us."

"What!" I shouted. "We are in the path of burning lava, molten rock and boiling water! We are going to be thrown into the air with hot ash, in a whirlwind of flames – and you say this is the best thing that can happen!"

"Yes," he replied, looking at me over the top of his glasses. "It is the only chance we have of returning to the surface of the Earth."

We went on rising all night. Towards morning, the temperature increased. The water had disappeared and the raft lay on a bed of lava, cooled by the air as we rose quickly. Hour after hour, the raft stopped and spun and rose. If Hans had not held me, my skull would have broken against the rocks. I remember little about the last few hours except for the sound of explosions and the speed of our raft spinning round and round. I shuddered and glanced at Hans's face and at the fire around us.

Then I closed my eyes and waited for death.

We came back to the surface of the Earth in Italy, through a volcanic eruption on the island of Stromboli. My uncle wrote about our journey and his book made him famous. My uncle became the happiest of scientists, and I became the happiest of men – when I married my little Gräuben.